Mountain Bikes & Garbanzo Beans

Beverly Lewis

Illustrated by Meredith Johnson

Augsburg
MINNEAPOLIS

To my dad, Herb Jones, who surprised me on my fifth birthday with a jazzy red English bike—my first set of wheels.

and

To my son Jonathan, whose middle name should've been bike, or at least rhyme with it . . . and who "eats" garbanzo beans in his salad, only if our dog Cuddles is begging nearby.

MOUNTAIN BIKES AND GARBANZO BEANS

Cover design: Hedstrom Blessing

Library of Congress Cataloging-in-Publication Data

Lewis, Beverly, 1949–
    Mountain bikes & garbanzo beans / by Beverly Lewis : illustrated by Meredith Johnson.
      p.   cm. — (Ready— set— read!)
    Summary: J.P. is very disappointed when the second-hand bike he hopes to buy gets sold to someone else, but helping a friend memorize Bible verses for a contest brings him new insights about sharing and forgiveness.
    ISBN 0-8066-2663-1 (permanent paper)
    [1. Bicycles and bicycling—Fiction.   2. Christian life—Fiction.]
I. Johnson, Meredith, ill.   II. Title.   III. Title: Mountain bikes and garbanzo beans. IV. Series.
PZ7.L58464Mo   1993
[Fic]—dc20   93-4606
                                                CIP
                                                AC

Manufactured in the U.S.A.   AF 9-2663

97   96   95   94   93   2   3   4   5   6   7   8   9   10

Contents

Veggies That
Never Die

J. P. Witmer pushed through his bottom dresser drawer. He slid his baseball cards aside. And the comic books.

His hand bumped the old cardboard box in the corner. The money box!

"J.P.," his mother called. "Your snack is ready."

"Oh, yuck," J.P. mumbled. He was sick of his mother's health kick. He was even having carrot and celery dreams. Bad dreams! Last night three giant carrots chased him to school.

J.P. emptied his pockets. He placed seven dollar bills in a row on his dresser.

Doing yardwork for his friend Shanna Parks' mom wasn't so bad after all. Only ten dollars to go, and Zeb Morgan's hot mountain bike was his!

J.P. stuffed his seven dollars inside the money box. He hid the box in the corner of the drawer. He spied a pack of bubblegum under some comic books.

Yes! How long had it been?

Weeks ago his mother had read some crazy health book. It was time for big changes, she'd said. Maybe it was okay for her, but J.P. was dying for sweets.

He stuffed four pieces of bubblegum in his mouth.

"J.P.," Mother called again.

Oops! The bubblegum had to go. Swallowing *this* much was stupid. J.P. saved his sugary wad. He stuck it on the gum wrapper and slammed the drawer shut.

"Coming," he answered.

Mother stood in the hallway with a tray of sliced carrots and celery sticks.

"Yuck," J.P. said, staring at the orange and green vegetables.

"Aren't you hungry?" Mother said, inching the tray closer.

"Not for *that* stuff."

"Have you been snitching sweets?"

J.P. shook his head. He had stuck to the diet. Anyway, gum didn't count.

J.P. took a handful of the orange and green health sticks. When his mother had gone, he pulled the junk drawer open again. He counted the money once more before hiding it in the box.

Inside a comic book was an envelope. He opened it and smelled the sweetness of strawberry fruit leather. His favorite!

Between bites of carrot and celery, J.P. stole three licks with his tongue. So he wouldn't forget the taste. He stashed the fruit leather back in the envelope. Then he stuffed his face with the wad of bubblegum.

Sneaking down the hallway, he hurried to find Zeb Morgan and his flashy mountain bike.

Ten Bucks
to Go

J.P. ran next door to Zeb's. Shanna Parks sat near the driveway watching some ants.

Zeb tossed a piece of wet cardboard in the trash. He picked up more trash in the garage.

"Hey, Zeb," called J.P.

Pushing the dark hair away from his face, Zeb said, "What's up?"

J.P. looked around. "How clean does your garage have to be?"

"Too clean. Enough to earn my allowance."

J.P. spotted the blue bike in the corner of Zeb's garage. "When are you getting your new bike?"

"Next week," Zeb said. "If you come up with the money for that old one. Then Grandpa will pay the rest."

"Only ten more dollars to go," J.P. said.

"That's a bagful," Zeb said. "How will you get it?"

J.P. watched Shanna let the ants crawl over her fingers on the sunny cement. "Hey, Shanna," called J.P. "Does your mom need any more help with the yard?"

"Don't know," Shanna said without looking up.

"Robin across the street might help you," Zeb said, leaning over the trash can. "She's good at thinking up stuff."

J.P. laughed. "Me, work with a girl?"

"You helped my mom," said Shanna. "She's a girl."

"That's different," J.P. muttered. He eyed Zeb's bike and moved towards it. *Ten more bucks*, he thought, touching the shiny frame. The golden flecks shone through the royal blue.

He could almost imagine speeding down the street on it. Of course, he'd have to learn to ride first. Even little Barbie Lou, his neighbor, could ride. She called him a baby last year when he tried but couldn't balance on two wheels.

"Catch you later," J.P. yelled. He crossed the street to Robin Demario's. Her father was outside shooting baskets.

Mr. Demario tossed the ball to J.P.

"Is Robin home?" J.P. asked.

"She's shopping with her mother," Mr. Demario said.

J.P. made a basket.

Across the street, Zeb hopped on his bike. He flew past Robin's house and down the street. *Where's he going so fast?* J.P. thought. He aimed the ball and shot. It bounced off the rim.

Mr. Demario's pager beeped. He rushed inside.

J.P. didn't like waiting around for a girl. Why couldn't *he* think of a way to earn the money? He didn't need Robin. Besides, it was late.

At home, J.P. pushed his salad around on his plate. The lettuce, sprouts, and garbanzo beans were yucky. When his mother wasn't looking, J.P. slipped the garbanzo beans to Muffie, his dog. She loved them.

The doorbell rang. J.P. raced to get it.

Zeb stood on the walk. He flipped the kickstand down on his bike. "Here's the deal. Another kid will give me five bucks more than you."

"Is that where you went so fast?" J.P. asked. He felt his neck grow warm.

"Yep," Zeb said. His wide brown eyes danced.

"But. . .but, I thought we had a deal," J.P. said, his breath coming fast. "You can't change your mind *now*."

Zeb stared at J.P. "Can you match it?"

"You want more money?" J.P. asked.

"*Here's* the deal." Zeb rubbed his fingers together. "Whoever's first with the bucks."

J.P. stared at the bike. *There's no way,* he thought. *I'm already ten dollars short.*

Dirty
Double-Cross

The next day, J.P. marched over to Robin Demario's after school.

He told her his plan to buy Zeb's mountain bike. And he told her about Zeb's deal—the *new* one.

Robin took off her glasses and cleaned them on her shirt. "Sounds like you need some quick money." She checked her glasses. "I know just the thing . . . a recycling project."

"A what?" J.P. asked.

"You know, a recycling project. Care for

the earth and pick up some extra cash at the same time. I'll call some kids to help."

"Perfect!" shouted J.P. "When do we start?"

Robin sat on the porch step. "Tomorrow's Saturday. Meet me in front of my house at eight."

"Gotcha." J.P. raced home to count his money one more time.

Saturday morning, J.P. and Robin met in front of her house. Barbie Lou pulled her red wagon. Shanna Parks wore her mother's garden gloves. Mark Tippett, Robin's cousin, showed up with armloads of trash bags.

"Are *all* of you helping?" J.P. asked.

Everyone nodded.

J.P. grinned. It felt good having so many friends.

Only Zeb was missing, but J.P. didn't care. He'd show Zeb all about good deals. He'd have the money soon. Maybe even today.

"If you buy Zeb's mountain bike, what will you do with it?" little Barbie teased.

"What do you think I'll do with it?" J.P. crossed his eyes at her.

Barbie screamed. "He's making faces."

Robin's cousin whistled with his fingers. "OK, you guys. We'll go to each house on our street. Then, to all the houses on Springflower Road. Robin and I will get old newspapers. Barbie and Shanna can pull the glass bottles in the wagon. J.P., you collect the aluminum cans." Mark gave J.P. a handful of heavy duty trash bags. "We'll split the total evenly."

Robin pushed up her glasses and grinned at Mark. "Let's go to Zeb's house first."

By lunch time, the kids had gathered a mountain of recyclable items. Enough to fill Mr. Demario's van. J.P., Mark, and Robin rode along to the recycling center.

On the way back, J.P. counted his share of the money. Fifteen dollars and forty-eight cents worth of work.

He dashed over to Zeb's. No one was home. So, J.P. went home and counted *all* his bike money. There was plenty.

Walking up and down the neighborhood had made J.P. hungrier than ever. At lunch, he ate his fish and salad without groaning. But he nearly choked on the garbanzo beans. Every other minute he excused himself to see if Zeb was home.

When his mother went to get more herbal tea, J.P. sneaked the last garbanzo beans to Muffie. She chomped them right down.

J.P. hurried to his room. He *had* to have a lick of strawberry fruit leather. Anything to get the taste of sprouts and garbanzo beans out of his mouth. He rooted through his junk drawer.

J.P. heard Zeb's grandpa drive up. He grabbed his money and slammed the drawer.

Zeb's grandpa pulled into the garage just as J.P. arrived.

"I've got the money," J.P. shouted, waving it. "*All* of it."

Zeb climbed out of the car. "Too late," he said. "The bike is sold."

J.P. stared at Zeb in the dimly lit garage. He was too stunned to speak.

Zeb dug his hand into his pocket, showing off the dollar bills. "Sorry, J.P. Someone beat you to it."

J.P. didn't know what to say. No way would he let double-crossing Zeb know there was a lump as big as a baseball in his throat.

4

Top Secret

J.P. sneaked in the back door. He tiptoed down the hall to his room. The floor squeaked.

"J.P.?" His mother called from the living room.

Phooey. He didn't want to talk to anybody right now.

J.P. felt like eating the strawberry fruit leather hidden in his junk drawer. He wished he had two hundred fruit leathers. And Jolly Ranchers and Almond Joys. Mom's health food diet was stupid. Who cared about being healthy anyway?

"J.P.?" came his mother's voice again.

He looked at the clock. *Oh, no,* he thought. *Time for the carrot and celery brigade.* Sure enough. Here came Mother with a full tray.

He scooped up a handful of each and waited until his mother's footsteps scuffled down the hallway. Then he lifted the mattress and stuffed the orange and green sticks underneath. *There.*

He headed for the junk drawer. He could almost taste the strawberry fruit leather.

The next morning, Robin's van left for church. J.P. watched as Robin, Shanna, and Barbie Lou climbed in. Mark, Robin's cool cousin, went too.

Robin had asked J.P. to go along. She was always asking. Mark, too. But J.P. was always able to think up an excuse. Excuses like he wasn't used to going to church or his dress-up clothes were too small.

"None of that matters," Robin had said. He was beginning to believe her.

J.P. sat outside on his porch steps feeling lonely. He stared over at Zeb's. He hoped the lousy double-crosser stayed inside all day. Now *there* was a kid for Robin's church.

J.P. was reading an old comic book when Robin's van finally arrived home. The page was torn where the strawberry leather had stuck. J.P. remembered how good that fruit leather tasted last night.

Robin came running across the street. "J.P.!"

"What's up?"

"Plenty," she said out of breath. "Can you hide something for me?"

J.P. cracked his fingers. "No problem."

Robin pulled a sandwich bag full of dollar bills from her purse.

"Wow," J.P. said. "That's a lot of money."

"For Mother's Day," Robin said. "It's top secret."

"Really?"

"Uh-huh." She handed the bag to J.P. "I can't hide it any more."

"How come?"

"I think someone's found my hiding place."

"Like who?"

"My baby brother," said Robin. "He's crawling now. And into everything."

"How do you know it's him?" J.P. asked.

"Every time I add my allowance to it, I can tell the dollars are slobbered on."

J.P. crossed his arms. "Your money is safe with me, Robin."

"Great!" She said. "Now I've got to brush these awful curls out and put on my jeans." She started to cross the street.

"How long do you want me to keep the money?" J.P. called.

"I'll come get it next Saturday when Dad and I go shopping for Mother's Day."

J.P. said, "It's a deal."

How's the bike *deal*?"

J.P. felt sick. "Oh, that."

Robin stopped in the middle of the street. "What do you mean?"

J.P. sat stone still.

"Where's the bike?" She said as she walked toward him.

"Zeb double-crossed me."

"How?"

"Sold it out from under my nose."

The Invitation

J.P. wished Robin would stop staring at him. He could see she wasn't leaving. Not until she heard it again.

"The bike is gone," J.P. repeated.

Robin sighed. "I'm sorry, J.P. I really am."

"It's not your fault," he said, cracking one knuckle after another.

"It's just too awful. I can't believe this."

Mark came around the corner dribbling his basketball. "Wanna play?"

"In a minute," Robin said.

He stopped dribbling. "You guys look like someone died."

Robin's lip drooped. "I think J.P. feels that way."

J.P. said, "You're a good pal, Robin."

"For a *girl* cousin, I guess she is," said Mark laughing. "Come on, J.P., let's go exploring."

Robin ran home for lunch.

Mark and J.P. headed for the far end of the street where a grove of pine trees made a mini-forest. Halfway into the woods, Mark leaned against a tree. He tossed his basketball to the ground and took out a black book. "See this?"

J.P. sat down on some pine needles.

"Robin's church gave me this on the first Sunday I went. I learned lots of verses from it. If I can say all of them by next Sunday, I'll win another ribbon. And then I'll have twenty-five ribbons. Maybe I'll even win the grand prize!"

J.P. was still thinking about Zeb's mountain bike.

"Here," Mark said. He handed the tiny New Testament to J.P. "Follow along and see if I've got it."

Mark began.

Halfway through, J.P. stopped him. "It's mixed up."

Mark started over. He missed more words.

"You were close, Mark." J.P. closed the book. "But I need to get home now. Mom's leafy lunch is calling."

Mark grinned. "Thanks, J.P. Can you help me again?"

"Sure," J.P. said, pushing himself up off the soft forest floor. He rubbed his hands on his jeans.

They walked back down their street. J.P. pushed his hands deep into his pockets. He felt Robin's money baggie. It was safe there.

30

"Why don't you come to church next Sunday?" said Mark. "It's Mother's Day. Bring your mom and get a rose."

J.P. scratched his head. "She'd like that."

When they walked past the Morgan's house, Zeb's mom was sitting by the window. Maybe *she* would like a rose on Mother's Day. But Zeb would have to go to Robin's church to get it. J.P.didn't feel much like asking *him*.

Mark darted across the street, his ball dancing under his leg. "Come over Wednesday after school," he called. "I'll have my verses ready by then."

"OK," said J.P. He didn't see what was so special about saying Bible verses from memory. Except maybe for the grand prize.

After lunch, he went to his room and opened his junk drawer. Robin's cash fit right into the cardboard money box. He stacked up a pile of baseball cards between Robin's money and his own. Her Mother's Day money was on the left and his bicycle money on the right.

He emptied his pockets of the garbanzo beans he'd sneaked off his plate. This health diet stunk. If Mom couldn't be more creative than garbanzo bean salads, he'd just have to hide them here in the junk drawer. They would be fine until trash day on Wednesday.

Mark Makes
a Deal

It was Monday.

J.P.'s class lined up for art. They were making pop-up heart vases from construction paper. For Mother's Day.

The art teacher asked Zeb to put a bottle of glue on each table. When he passed J.P.'s table, he bragged about his new dirt bike. He was getting it in two days.

J.P. felt sick. Everyone on his street owned a bike. Not only that, everyone could *ride* a bike. Even Barbie Lou.

Robin picked up some yellow construction paper next to her. It belonged to a new girl. Robin helped her follow the pattern, fold, and cut the pages.

J.P. watched Robin do what she did best—help others. He had to think of a way to thank her for helping him raise the money for Zeb's bike. Zeb's dumb old mountain bike.

The word was out by morning recess. Zeb had double-crossed J.P. Everyone knew. Even the first graders!

Bossy Barbie warned J.P. not to go near any chocolate bars with his left-over money. "You'll spoil your mother's plans for your health." she teased.

"Mind your own business." He turned away to look for the soccer game.

"It's not the *only* bike in the world, you know," Barbie said.

Maybe to her it wasn't. Maybe Barbie hadn't felt the smooth, shiny frame, its golden flecks smiling through the blue. Maybe she hadn't heard the whir of its jazzy tire spokes. She hadn't. . . .

The bell rang. Everyone raced to the school. Everyone except J.P. He dragged his feet.

Wednesday, after school, J.P. went straight home. He tossed left-over pieces of lettuce and three wrinkled garbanzo beans into the junk drawer. His money and Robin's money was safely hidden in the corner.

Then he headed to Mark's house to help him practice Bible verses.

Mark stood up straight, beside his desk.

J.P. sat on Mark's bed, checking the words in the tiny testament.

"Galatians 6:2: 'Carry each other's burdens, and in this way you will fulfill the law of Christ.' "

"That's right!" said J.P. "Now what?"

"Luke 3:11: 'The man with two tunics should share with him who has none, and the one who has food should do the same.' "

"You did it." J.P. handed the New Testament back. "Wow, I didn't know the Bible said things like that."

"Me either," said Mark, heading for the garage.

J.P. followed. "So, are you gonna do what it says?"

"Do what?" Mark reached for his basketball.

"You know, share some *real* food with me. Like it says in the Bible.

"Oh, no you don't." Mark laughed and shot two baskets. "I won't be responsible for messing with *your* mother's diet."

"It's a real yucky diet. Garbanzo beans and lettuce—junk like that." J.P. sat on an old bench in the corner. He watched Mark do his fancy footwork. *Zing!* In the ball went. A perfect shot.

"Your turn," Mark said.

"Are you gonna win the grand prize at church on Sunday?" J.P. asked.

"Hope so," Mark said whirling around and swishing the ball through the hoop.

"What's the prize?" J.P. asked.

"Hot new Rollerblades," Mark said out of breath.

"Really?" J.P. wiped his hands on his jeans and took a shot. In!

"That's what I'm trying for," Mark said, "I never ride my bikes anyway. I'm always playing ball, you know. But blading . . . well, I could practice basketball on them."

"Did you say *bikes*?" J.P. stopped bouncing the ball. "You have more than one?"

"Sure. You remember my ten-speed. Plus, my dad bought me a brand new BMX. I never ride either of them."

"Why not?"

"*This* is my life." Mark fired one up. The ball flew right through, without touching the rim.

J.P. had a new idea. He took a deep breath. "Want to sell one of them?"

Mark stopped playing. He wiped his face on his sleeve. "Hey, good idea. The ten-speed needs some paint. That's all."

"Great," decided J.P. "How much?"

"I'll take whatever you got." Mark dribbled the ball behind his back.

"I'll be right back," called J.P., hurrying home to get the money. He could trust Mark Tippett. If Mark said it, he meant it. He was no double-crosser.

Muffie!

J.P. flicked on his bedroom light. His room was a mess. Pajamas and towels were crumpled in a heap in the corner. The bed was lumpy. His dresser drawers yawned and jeans played peek-a-boo over the top.

J.P. kicked away pieces of gum wrapper with his foot.

Gum wrappers?

What were *they* doing out?

The junk drawer was junkier than ever. Scrambling to his knees, he pushed the comic books aside.

Searching, he felt for his bike money in the back of the drawer. There was a pile of baseball cards dividing his money on the right from Robin's on the. . . .

What?

Snibbles of scraps were all that was left of Robin's money! Bits of garbanzo beans were mixed in with the shredded dollar bills!

"What happened?" J.P. cried. "Who did this?"

A trail of the shredded mess led to the bathroom. Muffie whined and crouched in the corner of the shower.

J.P. wanted to shake her. No, that was too kind. He wanted to hang Muffie up by her floppy doggie ears.

"Muffie! How *could* you?"

J.P. slammed the bathroom door and looked in the mirror. "Can't you do anything right?" he yelled at his own face.

Muffie cried and crouched even more.

"It was those garbanzo beans. How stupid!" J.P. hit his head with his hand.

His mother knocked on the door. "J.P. are you all right?"

"No, I'm not. Robin's money is gone! Muffie ate it!"

"I can't understand what you are saying," his mother said.

"Everything is wrong. Robin counted on me and now. . . ."

J.P. picked up Muffie from the shower. Her breath smelled like beans.

"You little sneak," he hollered in the pooch's face. "I oughta' call the dog pound this minute!"

Muffie shook in J.P.'s arms as he carried her to the back door. As he set her outside, Muffie began to cry and whine. J.P. didn't care. He slammed the kitchen door and headed for his room.

The junk drawer sagged open. Half a garbanzo bean and some lettuce were scattered in the front . . . the reason for

Muffie's mischief. Deep inside, J.P. knew it was his own fault.

J.P. groaned. *If only I'd eaten them at mealtime. Those good-for-nothing beans!*

"J.P.," called his mother. "Your friend Robin is here. She wants to see you. She says it's about something top-secret."

His heart sank. She'd come for her Mother's Day money early.

J.P. fell onto his bed. He breathed fast and hard. How much money had she given him anyway?

On the floor behind the door he spied Robin's sandwich bag. The amount was written on a round pink sticker.

Twenty-two dollars!

There was only one thing to do.

He counted *his* money. It was *all* there. Down the street, Mark's ten-speed was just waiting to be his. Phooey!

J.P. stuffed his money into the sandwich bag. He would give it to Robin. She'd never have to know what happened to her half-eaten money. Or worse ... that he couldn't be counted on.

J.P. shuffled down the hall. *No bikes for a kid with a garbanzo bean freak for a dog!*

J.P. swallowed the lump in his throat. "I'm coming."

8

Two Lies
in One Day

After Robin left, the phone rang.

"Where *are* you?" Mark asked. "I thought you were coming right back to buy the ten-speed."

"I was, but . . ." J.P. stopped. "Mom is real sick and she needs me here." It was a lie.

"OK," Mark said. "Tomorrow after school then?"

"Uh, uh . . . no. I can't come over then." J.P. made up another story. "Robin's helping me with a science project."

"What project?" Mark asked. "I didn't know about one."

"I . . . I . . . uh, have to go."

J.P. felt lousy. He'd lied to Mark. Twice. The next day, J.P. stayed away from Mark at first recess. Finally, Mark cornered him by the door in the afternoon.

"Hey, J.P. You're acting strange. What's wrong?"

J.P.'s face felt hot. His hands were sweaty. "I guess I don't lie very well."

"Lie?" Mark scratched his head. He looked puzzled.

J.P. stumbled over his words. "I lied . . . about . . . about why I didn't buy your ten-speed."

"You did?"

He didn't want to tell Mark about Muffie eating Robin's money. He didn't want her to find out. She would think he couldn't be counted on.

"It's a long story, and you'd never believe it anyway."

"It's OK, J.P.," Mark said. "Really it is. You don't *have* to buy it. I just thought you. . . ."

"But, I *do* want your bike. More than anything."

"So what's the problem?" Mark asked.

"I'll tell you if you keep it quiet."

Mark nodded. "Scouts honor."

"No foolin?" J.P. begged for a promise.

"No foolin."

J.P. told the truth this time. Everything.

Mark stared at J.P. "You used your *own* money? So Robin wouldn't know hers got eaten by Muffie?"

J.P. pulled out his pocket linings. "See? I'm broke."

"Let's get this straight," Mark said. "You gave Robin the money you made from our recycling project? The bucks that were gonna buy you some wheels?"

"It wasn't easy to do, but that's the *true* story."

48

"Wow! That is some act of charity."

"Huh?" J.P. cracked his knuckles.

"Charity. You know . . . kindness. When you give because you care." Mark pushed his hair back.

"Sounds like a Mother's Day card," J.P. joked.

"Hey, no kidding, we talked about it in Sunday school last week."

"Yeah?" J.P. said. "You talk about stuff like that?"

"Sure. Have you ever heard this before: 'It is better to give than to receive'?"

J.P. snapped his fingers. "Some wise old saying?"

Mark smiled. "Better than wise. It's in the Bible."

"Along with those verses about sharing food and stuff like that?" J.P. asked.

Mark grinned.

"Gotcha," said J.P.

"See you at church this Sunday?"

"And hear you say your verses about sharing and feeding kids on dumb diets?" added J.P. "I can't miss that."

"Bring your mother and get a rose." Mark said.

The bell rang and J.P. hurried inside.

He wondered how he could pass a good feeling like this on to Zeb, the double-crosser. The new dirt bike owner, the. . . .

Mrs. Shelton interrupted J.P.'s thoughts. "Please turn to page 118, class. Begin by solving problem number one. And be sure to show your work."

J.P. couldn't believe his eyes. The math problem was about four boys in a marathon bike race!

The Contest

It was a sunny Mother's Day.

J.P. and his mother went to Robin's church. In Sunday school, the pastor gave him a New Testament. Like Mark's.

J.P. crossed his fingers when Mark said his verses. "He did it," said J.P.

Robin clapped her hands. "He's terrific!"

J.P. liked Robin. For a girl, she was a good friend.

"Now for the grand prize," Robin whispered. She took her place beside Mark and three others. Mark was up against four girls.

J.P. heard each verse. They were better than wise old sayings. He looked down at his New Testament. He held it with both hands.

What a close round! J.P. cracked his knuckles and hoped Mark would win.

Back to Robin. She was good at saying her verses. She oughta be, thought J.P. She'd been at it all her life. It was different for Mark. He was new at this.

The final round came. J.P. watched each girl wrinkle her nose or twist her hair before reciting the verse.

One girl forgot the chapter and verse but said the book of the Bible. She was out.

Her mistake was catching. The other girls forgot a word.

Mark looked relaxed. Was he thinking about basketball? The grand prize?

Squeezing his New Testament, J.P. rooted for Mark.

"Mark Tippett," the teacher said. "Say Luke 3:11."

Mark paused. He looked at the ceiling.

J.P. wanted to crack his knuckles as fast as he could. He waited. *C'mon, Mark, you can do it.*

Even J.P. remembered this one. It was a great verse! The one about sharing junk food with a kid on a health diet.

The teacher looked at her stop watch. "Five seconds."

J.P.'s heart leaped. The air was tense. The suspense was too much.

The teacher started to raise her hand just as Mark began, " '. . . the man with two tunics should share them with him who has none, and the one who has food should do the same.' Luke 3:11."

Robin was next. She looked at the teacher. J.P. thought she held her breath.

The teacher said another verse. Robin had to tell where it was found. Tricky.

There was a long silence. Robin turned to Mark. "I don't know for sure."

"You have five seconds," the teacher said, again.

Robin looked up, she looked down. She shook her folded hands.

"Time's up," came the teacher's voice.

Mark was the grand prize winner! Everyone clapped for Mark . . . and Robin.

Robin was second. Her eyes danced as she shook Mark's hand.

J.P. shot her a "thumbs up."

"Thanks," Robin said as she sat down.

Mark took a seat beside J.P. "She's a winner at losing," Mark whispered. "Some great cousin."

"No kidding. Now what?"

"The grand prize!"

10

A Grand
Surprise

J.P. opened the door for Mark as he loaded his grand prize into the van. Inside, they opened the box to check out the slick new Rollerblades. Robin and Barbie leaned over the seat for a closer look.

"Wow! They're something else!" said Robin.

"How many verses total?" asked Robin's father.

Mark grinned. "Twenty-five."

"Amazing," said J.P.'s mom, holding two Mother's Day roses.

J.P.'s stomach growled. "I'm starved," he said.

His mother's face beamed. "There's a surprise in the oven," she said.

"Real food, I hope?"

"How does meatloaf sound for a change?" she said.

"I don't believe it," J.P. said. "That's too cool."

Barbie grinned. "That's how Zeb talks."

Mark stuffed his fancy Rollerblades back in the box. "I've been thinking, J.P. What if I *give* you my ten-speed?"

"You would *do* that?" said J.P.

"Sure," said Mark. He pushed the lid down. "I've got what I want right here." He tapped on the box. "And in here." He patted his chest.

"Huh?" J.P. questioned.

"The verses aren't just in my head anymore. They're in my heart, too."

J.P. held his New Testament. He was beginning to understand what Mark meant.

Mark tapped his fingers on top of the grand prize box. "Luke 3:11—Mark Tippett's way—says: If you have two bikes, which I do, share with J.P. who doesn't have even one."

Robin laughed. "Mark might make a good preacher," she said as Mr. Demario turned the corner to their street.

J.P. cracked his knuckles. "This is the best Mother's Day ever."

His mother smiled. "Thank you for inviting us," she said to Robin's parents.

"Come with us any time," said Robin with a sparkle in her eye.

"Next Sunday?" J.P. asked.

"Yeah!" cheered Mark, climbing out of the van. "Hey, come over after dinner and pick up your ten-speed."

"Check with your parents first," J.P.'s mom said.

"Hey, what's your hurry?" J.P. called to Mark.

"I have a Mother's Day rose to deliver," Mark shouted over his shoulder.

J.P. crossed the street with his mother. "Happy Mother's Day, Mom," he said.

"Thanks, J.P." She smelled the roses then handed him one. "I know we must have gotten two of these for a reason."

J.P. held the front door open for her. He smelled the oven dinner. "No bean salad today?"

"It's time for a change," she said.

"All right!" J.P. shouted, heading to Zeb's.

Next door, Zeb's house was noisy with his grandpa's lawn mower. Zeb was fooling with fancy blue spokes on his new bike.

"Hi, Zeb." J.P. held out a long-stemmed rose.

"Whatcha got?" Zeb asked.

"Give it to your mom for Mother's Day."

"Hey thanks, man." Zeb looked surprised. "Where'd it come from?"

"Robin's church."

"Thanks," Zeb said again. "That's cool."

J.P. cracked two knuckles. "How do you like your new bike?"

"It's OK, but I miss my old one."

"Really?"

"I wish I'd kept it. Or sold it to you. It's a piece of junk now. You would have treated it better than *that* kid does."

J.P. didn't know what to say. Before today he might have felt secretly glad. Glad that Zeb messed up by selling his bike to someone else. Someone who didn't take care of it.

But not today. Things were different.

"Well, I gotta go."

"What's your hurry, man?" Zeb asked, jumping up.

"Got a lunch date with my mother."

"For Mom's Day?" Zeb asked. He held the rose stem carefully between two thorns.

"Uh-huh. She makes a mean meatloaf."

"Sounds nasty," Zeb muttered.

J.P. heard. It didn't matter. Meatloaf sure beat garbanzo beans anytime. Any day.

And bikes? Well, Mark owned two of them. And thanks to Luke 3:11, one would be his.